I0470413

Grégori Coudert

20 YEARS OF
FINANCIAL
MARKETS

Understand the reaction of financial
markets to economic and social
events

Copyright © 2019 Grégori Coudert
All rights reserved
Paris - FRANCE
ISBN: 9781071397701

ACKNOWLEDGEMENTS

First of all, I would like to thank here the research assistant Lisa Langevin who worked with me to build this book on the fluctuations of the financial markets over the last twenty years. Her attention to detail and her reflection on the text were very helpful.

I also thank the many friends who read the first drafts of this book and with whom I was able to discuss the subject.

Finally, I dedicate this book to this finance professional who worked in the World Trade Center, with whom I was in daily contact and more particularly on September 11, 2001 and of whom I have never heard again.

Foreword

Why this book?

This book is a practical tool for monitoring stock market investments and understanding the relationship between exogenous events and financial market fluctuations. It provides a chronological overview of economic trends and incidents that have affected global markets over the past twenty years.

This book is intended for students, people wishing to learn more about the financial markets and financial professionals. Students will find the main economic trends they need to know and their influences on financial markets. Individuals will be able to better understand and synthesize past events that have impacted their investments. Finally, financial professionals will find it interesting to immerse themselves in these periods they have been through with joy or sorrow. For the latter, this book also represents a methodical help on past economic events that tend to disappear from their memory.

How to read this book?

There are many definitions of financial markets in the books or on the Internet, but what do they actually represent?

Financial markets are the meeting of the opinion and decision-making of millions of investors who converge at a single point to give the value (the price) of an asset (stock, index, commodities, bonds, etc.).

Over the past twenty years, there have been major trends of contraction and expansion of economic activity in developed and emerging countries. The impact of these changes is decisive since they fundamentally affect the valuations of companies and therefore those of global stock market indices.

In addition to these fundamental movements, we can distinguish certain specific events, such as attacks, health or natural disasters... These events often benefit from extensive media coverage that increases the psychological importance of the event, but blurs investors' perceptions and the importance of the event's impact on companies. These accidents increase the level of volatility of financial assets but often have only a limited impact on the valuation of companies.

The two parts of the book begin with a graphical curve of the evolution of the main world financial indices. In the first part, the curve is divided into five main trends, followed by the texts explaining them. In the second part, the graph is annotated when volatility increases (peaks and sharp drops) and the cross-references explain these erratic movements.

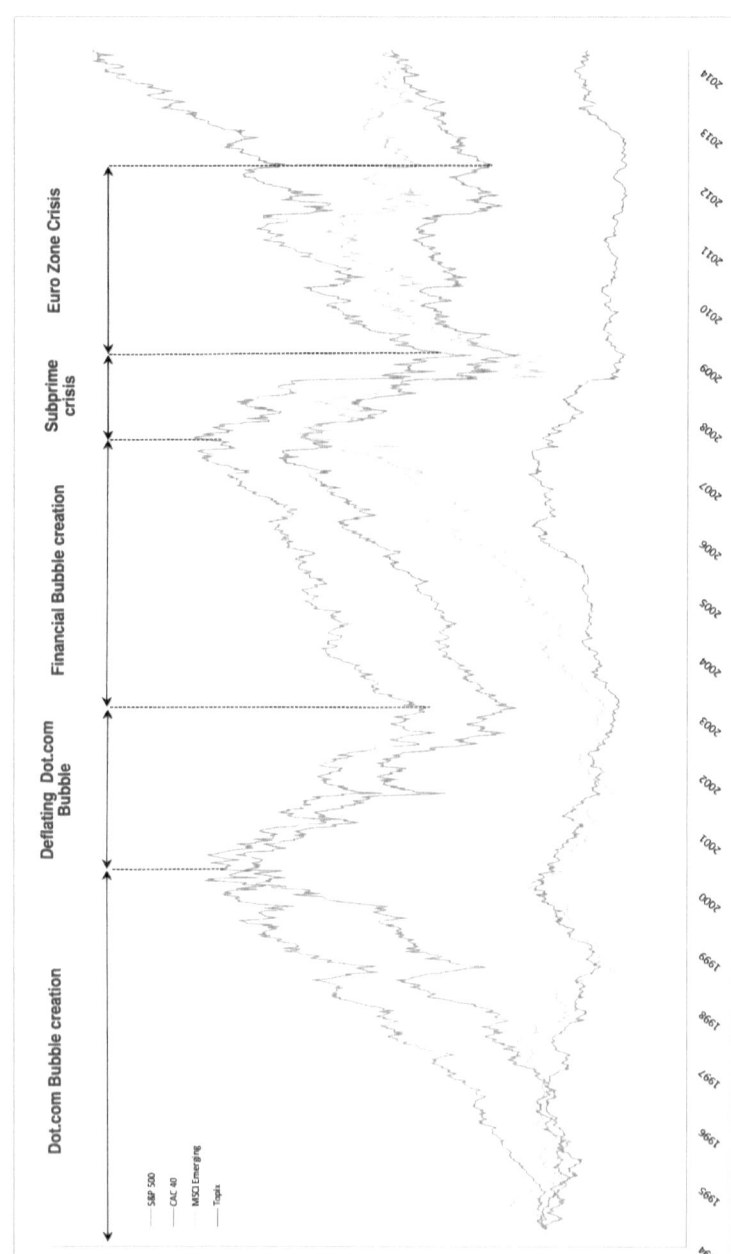

PART I.

INFLUENCE OF MAJOR ECONOMIC TRENDS ON FINANCIAL MARKETS

I. Of the new economy to the creation of the internet bubble

The technology bubble, also known as the dot.com bubble, is a speculative bubble[1], formed in the mid-1990s.

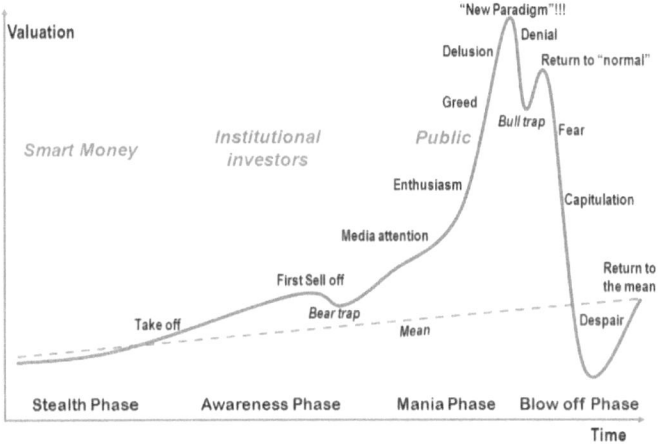

Source: Jean-Paul Rodrigue, Dept of Economics & Geography, US 2008

The last financial bubble of the 20th century began in the early 1990s: it is called the technology bubble, or " dot.com bubble". First, it affects the equity market for "new technology stocks". The fields

---

[1] Speculative bubble: it is a peak in the valuation of an asset caused by strong demand. The bubble is seen in the collapse of demand and therefore of valuation.

concerned are those related to information technology, telecommunications, media and information technology, which were developing very strongly at the time. This new sector of activity is called the TMT sector (Techno, Media, Telecom). This hysteria of growth in the new technologies sector then spread to other areas of activity. The most obvious example is that of Compagnie Générale des Eaux (CGE), a former utility company (water distribution, waste collection, transport) which will become in a few years under the leadership of its CEO Jean-Marie Messier (J2M) a global conglomerate mainly oriented towards the media: Vivendi.

In the United States, at the beginning of the 1990s, there was a significant development of start-ups in the field of TMT. This phenomenon is spreading rapidly in Europe, with investors being particularly keen on these new investment opportunities heralding the digital industrial revolution.

A. The beginnings of the development of the Internet bubble

In 1995, the first signs of the bubble's development were observed, with the IPO of Netscape, the web browser that dominated the market in the mid-1990s. In the second half of the decade, it became the most widely used browser. At the time of its initial public offering, the Netscape share price rose from $28 to $75 in a single day, an increase of 167%. Competing with Internet Explorer, Netscape will disappear in 2008 following the "Browser War".

Over the next 5 years, until 2000, investors participated massively in the development of the TMT sector. The growth of the sector requires capital, which generates a large volume of equity, bond and bank credit issues to finance the industrial revolution. IPOs[2] arrived in large quantities on the equity markets, to finance these companies in search of capital on the one hand and on the other hand to meet the growing demand of euphoric investors, in search of the right deal, i.e. the future Oracle or Microsoft. A real imbalance is then created between the increase in the market value of these new companies and their economic performance.

---

[2] IPO: "Initial Public Offering": listing of a company's share on the stock exchange.

Financial valuations continue to increase. For example, the NASDAQ index[3], which was 1000 points at the beginning of 1995, has increased fivefold in five years, reaching 5000 points.

B. Factors driving the development of the Internet bubble

From 1995 onwards, the development of the Internet bubble accelerated, for several reasons:

❖   In most OECD countries, the telecommunications market is opening up to competition and growing with the increase in the volume of data transferred daily. This has the effect of reorganizing this new sector, resulting in numerous mergers and acquisitions and financing needs,

❖   the population of developed countries is increasingly acquiring mobile phones, computers and computer equipment of all kinds (printers, personal assistants, etc.)

❖   the development and use and advent of the Internet network from 1994 onwards,

❖   the changeover to the euro and the changeover to the year 2000. In 1999, companies invested in adapting their information systems to ensure their exchanges in the financial markets and to bring their accounting into compliance,

❖   Monetary policy is favorable in the United States and Japan with low interest rates that encourage investment and debt,

❖   the world population at the time had a financial savings surplus, due to the retirement savings of the baby boomers,

---

[3] NASDAQ: "National Association of Securities Dealers Automated Quotations". NASDAQ is the second largest equity market in the United States, in terms of volume traded after the New York Stock Exchange. This market is specialized in new technology companies

❖ the increase in stock option plans[4], which favorized employees, has also led to major financial scandals, such as the Enron and WorldCom cases in 2001. In the United States, the Sarbanes-Oxley Act will put an end to these abuses by providing greater financial transparency and control. In 2003, Bill Gates announced the end of Microsoft's stock option plans, which had allowed the company's first employees to enrich themselves substantially at all levels of the company,

❖ financial analysts have overvalued new technology companies (see paragraph on the deflation of the financial analysts' technology bubble crash),

❖ the use of the goodwill valuation method: goodwill, is a valuation difference between the purchase price of a company and its fair value under IFRS. For example, if a company buys another one for 100 million euros when its economic value is only 80 million euros then the goodwill will be 20 million euros. This phenomenon had a strong impact on the creation of the technology bubble: investors overbought companies that were making losses but for which they had high expectations in terms of profits. Subsequently, these companies had to write off these valuation differences in their accounts, using the goodwill valuation method, which consists in adjusting their asset value to take into account their real economic profitability.

The peak of this technology bubble was in March 2000, with a NASDAQ index peaking at 5,048 points. In France, France Telecom quoted 200 euros in March 2000 and will lose 97% of its value to quote 7 euros in September 2002.

---

[4] Stock options: see definition in the appendix

II. The deflation of the technology bubble

A. Course of events

The deflation of the technology bubble can be broken down into four different phases.

1. The runaway phase (fall 1999 - spring 2000)

The enthusiasm linked to the development of new technologies is accelerating the rise in stock prices. Investors, without any discernment, no longer make a selection among companies, but buy NASDAQ or CAC 40 indices on a massive scale, because the performance of these indices (composed largely of new technology companies) is excellent. It's the gold rush: all stocks are rising, and wealth is guaranteed for all. At the same time, Time Warner, a publishing, film production and television company, was acquired by AOL, reassuring investors in their belief in the domination of new technology companies.

But many companies have a negative economic result. Investors are realizing that not only are profits not turning positive, but losses are increasing. In addition, expenses are still high, and revenues are not on the rise as promised in the business plans. The main reason is due to a gap between the consumer and his consumption habits in the face of these new services and products.

2. The doubt phase (spring to autumn 2000)

During this phase, some unusual events occur, such as:

❖ the France Telecom share gains 20% in a single day. This increase, linked to the IPO of its Internet subsidiary Wanadoo, is beginning to raise doubts among investors. The title is too largely overbought.

❖ the share of Global Crossing (an American optical fiber telecommunications company founded at the end of 1997) lost about 60% of its value in a few weeks, creating a first shock for investors. The sharp drop is due to an awareness among some investors of the financial viability of this type of company and an excessive valuation of its assets compared to its competitors.

These two events, although worrying, do not yet affect investor confidence: prices remain at their highest level. The CAC 40 even reached a record high on September 4, 2000 at 6944 points. In parallel, other mergers and acquisitions are taking place in the sector, such as Vivendi's merger with Canal+ and Seagram.

3. The stagnation phase (November 2000 - November 2001)

The few fears sown by the incoherent events of the doubt phase are beginning to emerge: investors are stopping their frenzy and starting to slow down their purchases of securities linked to new technologies. They realize that profits are not forthcoming, that losses are increasing and are sometimes multiplied.

In the end, these new companies are proving less profitable than previously thought. Analysts have issued overly optimistic medium-term forecasts and debt seems too high compared to corporate profitability.

In addition, costly mergers and acquisitions, combined with excessive operating expenses, mean that profits do not take off as promised in business plans and add to already heavy debts. Finally, these companies are having difficulty repaying their debts, which will get seriously worse when the Fed's key rates start to rise.

INFLUENCE OF KEY RATES: key rates are set by the central bank of a monetary union or country. They enable the bank to regulate economic activity and inflation. The bank thus influences the cost of credit and the return on liquidity. The country's various banks deposit their money with the central bank, which pays interest on the deposit at a certain rate it sets. The lower the rate of return on deposits, the less likely banks are to leave their money with the central bank and the more they will lend to businesses and households. Through this mechanism, central banks use this rate to stimulate or slow down the country's growth and consumption.

---

4. The panic phase (from December 2001 to February 2003)

On December 2, 2001, Enron (a company specializing in energy and raw materials) went bankrupt. Thanks to complex arrangements and fraudulent schemes by its CEO, the company had succeeded in concealing its losses and misleading investors (see paragraph on major fraudulent schemes). Investors are panicking, while other major groups are going bankrupt: Winstar Communications, Viatel, Global TeleSystems ... When in doubt, investors try to sell their high-tech securities, causing their prices to fall massively. On October 9, 2002, the Nasdaq reached its lowest level in ten years.

The economic recession then begins in this sector and spreads to the economy in general. For example, the cumulative profits of companies listed on the NASDAQ between 1995 and 2000 give way to an equivalent loss in just a few months. In the United States, about 210 new technology companies are going bankrupt. Among them, only a few will manage to maintain their activity: Google, Yahoo, eBay, Amazon.

The stock market crash announces the end of the internet bubble. The CAC 40 lost more than half its value in two years: it collapsed to 2400 points on March 12, 2003 from 6944 points in September 2000. The three most indebted companies, France Telecom, Vivendi and Alcatel, each lost more than 90% of their value in 2002. Their CEOs complain about credit rating agencies[5], which give them poor ratings. For example, Standard & Poor's downgraded Vivendi in 2002, downgrading it from an "investment" (low-risk) to an unenviable "speculative" (or junk bond) category. The consequence of downgrading a rating is an increase in the group's access to financing: riskier companies borrow at higher credit rates. These rating changes are justified but come too late, it would have been appropriate to have a gradual downgrade of ratings as debt increases and the financial health of companies deteriorates, rather than at the bottom of the equity markets. This mistake will happen again during the subprime crisis.

---

[5] Definition and role of credit rating agencies in the appendix

13

B. Factors aggravating the crisis

From the 2000s onwards, the crisis revealed fraudulent maneuvers by a few companies and unscrupulous financial analysts, contributing to the loss of confidence and the stock market crash.

1. Major fraud schemes

Enron was a listed company specializing in natural gas and electricity brokerage. With the creation of thousands of offshore companies by the group's CEO, Jeffrey Skilling, in tax havens, Enron transformed its loans into commercial contracts. This made it possible to boost the group's results and reduce credit risks. These loans were secured by the Enron share. When the markets fell, the partner banks had to request compensation or repayments because of the decline in the Enron share, which no longer covered the guarantees, resulting in the reappearance of significant debts in the group's accounts.

In addition, in agreement with the audit firm Arthur Andersen, the gas was recorded at market value and not at historical value. This method made the group's results very volatile (see graph of gas prices in the United States). In the fall of 2001, the CEO sold his Enron shares massively, while their value was falling, and at the same time encouraged his employees to buy them, making them believe that the stock was rebounding. With the fall in gas prices, which mechanically depressed results, and the reintegration of debt into the group's balance sheet, Enron, stranded, went bankrupt in December 2001, taking the Arthur Andersen firm with it.

US gas index
($/baril)

Source: www.eia.gov

WorldCom, the second largest telephone operator in the United States, went bankrupt in 2002, leaving more than $40 billion in debt. Its CEO, Bernard Ebbers, will be sentenced to 25 years in prison for carrying out the biggest accounting fraud in American history, by fictitiously increasing his company's turnover by more than 10 billion dollars. Indeed, the judges criticize him for having ordered the falsification of his company's accounts from the summer of 2000, when the telecoms sector was beginning to suffer from the crisis resulting from the bursting of the internet bubble. Arthur Andersen, already involved in the Enron case, was the company's auditor. This fraud will remain the largest in American history until Madoff's fraud in 2008.

2. The crash of financial analysts

Before the Internet bubble was created, analysts worked in the shadows. Their mission was to decipher, through balance sheets, income statements and information meetings with companies, the true financial health of the latter. But with the financialization of the economy and the growing demand for financial information, analysts became the "only competent interpreters" of corporate accounts.

Their role is then more and more important, they take a prominent place in the economic and financial landscape and strongly influence the choice of fund managers and investors in general. This eventually leads to abuses: in May 2002, the SEC[6] conducted about ten investigations into the accounts of unscrupulous financial analysts.

To cite a few examples:

❖ the World Com action had been strongly recommended by Jack Grubman, an analyst at Salomon Brothers Bank and a friend of the WorldCom CEO. He was later banned from the profession,

❖ New York State Attorney Eliot Spitzer will prosecute analysts and brokers for conflicts of interest, which will be sanctioned by fines for financial fraud,

❖ in France, some analysts are accused of supporting Jean-Marie Messier, Vivendi's CEO at the time, who had disseminated false information about the company's financial statements,

❖ finally, new, less traditional methods of business valuation are emerging to "adapt" to the new economy. Through these valuation methods, analysts transform loss-making companies into investment opportunities. Thus, the three leading players in the CAC 40, France Telecom, Vivendi and Alcatel, will make huge losses due to the depreciation of Goodwill on investments made in previous years. Goodwill becomes Bad will, i.e. a loss. These losses will oblige France Telecom's main shareholder, the French State, to support the company and to carry out a capital increase.

The decline in the various stock market values reveals a lack of confidence following the various scandals and unreasonable valuations of certain companies. The crisis is spreading throughout the economy and companies are struggling to find capital. In addition, investors, especially small investors, lose a large share of

---

[6] SEC: Securities and Exchange Commission. The U.S. federal agency responsible for the supervision and regulation of financial markets. It can be compared to the AMF (Autorité des Marchés Financiers) in France.

their equity investments. This mistrust leads to a generalized fall in stock market indices, affecting all sectors of the economy.

The deflation of the technology bubble and the stock market decline will continue until March 2003.

III. Creation of the financial bubble

A. The return to growth of financial markets

From March 2003, we are witnessing a return to an upward trend in the financial markets that will continue until the beginning of summer 2007. This reversal is mainly due to the market purge from 2000 to 2003, the restructuring of corporate accounts and technology stocks in particular, a return to normal valuation levels and the decline in key rates by the Fed.

This return to growth accelerated from June 2003. On June 25, the President of the American Central Bank, Alan Greenspan, who had already been engaged in a policy of lowering key rates since early 2001, finally lowered the Fed's key rate to 1%. The purpose of this decline is to revive a faltering economy and to stem the dramatic fall in financial markets. Moreover, with historically low rates in 2003, global growth is picking up, driven at the same time by high growth rates in emerging countries and China in particular, but also by speculation, with institutional investors benefiting from abundant and cheap liquidity.

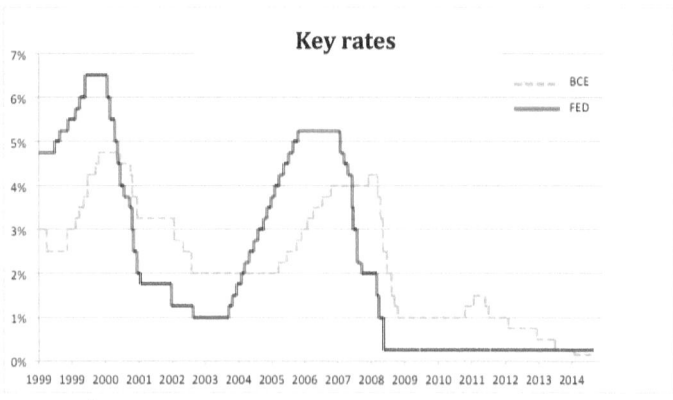

Source: www.ecb.europa.eu

During this period, all banks around the world developed their investment banking business, which proved extremely profitable. For example, in France, only Société Générale was specialized in this field. The so-called "network" banks are also developing this expertise, such as Crédit Agricole with the purchase of Crédit Lyonnais, or BNP with the takeover of Paribas in 2000. In parallel with these external growths, they are developing their CIB (Corporate and Investment Banking) department, which began to develop in the 1990s.

From 2004, the banks' economic performance literally exploded and the financial sector (including banks, insurance, financial holding companies and financial services) became the leading sector of stock market indices, accounting for around 40% of the CAC 40 index and 50% of the Spanish IBEX index at the height of the financial bubble.

B. The creation of the real estate bubble in the United States

In June 2012, President George W. Bush set the goal of increasing the number of first-time homeowners to more than 5 million households by granting billions of dollars in tax credits and subsidies. Freddie Mac and Fannie Mae[7], authorized to lend and guarantee loans from other financial institutions, have pledged $440 billion to guarantee the state-initiated "Neighbor Works America" organization for minority home ownership.

At the same time, banks are beginning to grant more and more home loans to individuals: between 2002 and 2003, the refusal rate for home loans in the United States was only 14%, half the rate observed in 1997. This leads to an increase in property prices, with a 10% increase over the same period. The states most affected by this increase are the most populated: California, Florida and the North-Eastern States.

After the Fed cut the key rate to 1%, encouraging banks to lend to individuals, we are witnessing a historic record number of homebuyers close to 70% in the United States. Fannie Mae and Freddie Mac then bought $434 billion in bonds linked to subprime loans.

---

[7] Fannie Mae and Freddie Mac: see definition in appendix

DEFINITION OF SUBPRIMES: SUBPRIMES are subprime loans characterized by a combination of variable and fixed interest rates granted to low-income households. In return for more flexible allocation criteria than for traditional loans, the interest payable is higher. To make credit attractive to the borrower, banks and specialized credit agencies offer low rates at the beginning of the loan (during the first two years), then a sharp increase in the rate thereafter. These loans represent a higher overall rate for the borrower and a higher return for the lender to compensate for the risk of default. Par elsewhere, this risk is generally limited by the mortgage guarantee taken on the borrower's home: if the borrower can no longer meet the repayment deadlines for his mortgage, the lender reimburses himself on the resale of the home.

To avoid having to pay high interest rates, borrowers sold their homes before the two-year maturity date and received the significant capital gain realized through the rise in the real estate market.

In October 2004, the SEC (Security and Exchange Commission) suspended the prudential rules governing capital for five major firms: Goldman Sachs, Merrill Lynch, Lehman Brothers, Bear Stearns and Morgan Stanley. Previously, these banks had to keep a significant portion of their equity capital (a certain amount set aside for security) in order to grant a loan.

Freed from regulatory limits on their indebtedness, the leverage rate of the five major firms increases very sharply to 20, 30 or even 40 to 1. This modification of the capital rules will make it possible to multiply exponentially the amount and number of loans, and consequently the size of their balance sheet.

The housing bubble then began to grow: in 2004-2005, Arizona, California, Florida, Hawaii and Nevada saw record price increases of more than 25% per year.

In September 2005, the use of leverage[8], which has high profitability and induces a high level of risk, was extended to small

---

[8] Leverage effect: see appendix

banks. Indeed, the Federal Reserve, the FDIC[9] and the OCC[10] allow the reduction of mandatory reserves for small banks, allowing them to go into debt, which was only possible for the five main big banks. This phenomenon further encourages the development of home loans.

While the European banking landscape is concentrated, in the United States there are a very large number of small banks. A banking network can be made up of only two or three branches. During the financial crisis, these hundreds of small banks will go bankrupt.

Finally, in the fall of 2005, the real estate market boom came to a sudden end. From the last quarter of 2005 to the first quarter of 2006, median national prices began to decline slowly (-3.5% over the period) and then the correction accelerated until January 2009.

Source: www.spindices.com, S&P Case Shiller Index[11]

---

[9] FDIC: Federal Deposit Insurance Corporation. A U.S. federal agency whose primary responsibility is to guarantee bank deposits made in the United States up to a certain amount.

[10] OCC: Office of the Controller of the Currency. An independent office within the U.S. Treasury that regulates and supervises all domestic banks.

[11] S&P case Shiller Index: index measuring the market value of residential real estate in twenty metropolitan areas of the United States

IV. The subprime crisis and the deflation of the bubble

From 2006 onwards, there was a significant slowdown in the real estate market. Prices are stagnating, the volume of home sales is falling, and the stock is increasing. At the same time, the new construction index fell by 40% compared to 2005.

Subprime loans accounted for 24% of new home loans in 2006. As demand for real estate decreases, the value of these properties decreases, leading at the same time to a decrease in the wealth of borrowers. In the United States, homeowners can borrow for consumer credit based on the value of their property. The more value the good adds, the more they can consume. On the other hand, the decline in the value of the property reduces their ability to consume. Consumption accounts for 60% of the United States' Gross Domestic Product.

A. The causes of the subprime crisis

The subprime crisis was initiated and then reinforced by various factors.

1. The rise in interest rates initiated by the Fed

The interest rates on subprime loans are floating-rates. They were initially set on the basis of the Fed's key rates, which were low at the time. But from 2004 to the end of 2006, the Fed raised its rates from 1% to 5.25%. This reversal, which was probably too fast, trapped mainly floating-rates indebted households and slowed too sharply the growth of the real estate sector, which is essential for developed economies.

WHY THIS RAPID RISE IN KEY INTEREST RATES? This is due to the growth of the American economy. Growth leads to an increase in prices and therefore a decrease in the value of the currency: this is inflation. To combat a sharp increase in inflation, the main tool is monetary policy, through the setting of key rates.

In the United States, the Fed decides to raise its key rates to limit inflation. In doing so, the Fed influences the main financial institutions (banks and credit institutions), which in turn increase their commercial interest rates, granted to households and businesses. Rising bank interest rates are slowing household and business demand. Slower demand drives down prices, leading to lower inflation.

2. Securitization of receivables

Banks and credit institutions, freed from regulatory limits (see p. 20) on their debt, securitize part of their receivables in order to make them more liquid.

SECURITIZATION MECHANISM: banks, which issue loans, create intermediary companies in which these loans constitute assets. In return for these assets, the bank issues bonds, which constitute the liabilities of these intermediary companies. The interest and loan repayments are then used to pay interest on the bonds issued and to repay them. The main interest of securitization is to monetize (make liquid and exchangeable) initially illiquid private and commercial movable assets.

Banks convert their receivables into securities issued on the financial markets in the form of bonds. These bonds, called ABS (Asset Backed Securities) and CDO (Collateralized Debt Obligations)[12], are offered to investors and offer attractive rates of return. When households began to lose the ability to repay their

---

[12] ABS and CDO bonds: see appendix

home loans, these popular securities became riskier and began to decline in value.

The more lenders securitize their receivables, the more equity they have to provide new loans. Securitization makes it possible to remove loans from the balance sheet of these financial institutions and thus to free up equity capital for new loans. In addition, securitized subprime loans are mixed with other financial products such as consumer credit and then re-securitized again on a global scale. As a result of these stacks of loans, it had become difficult to know which securitized product held subprime-related investments and in what quantities.

3. The change in accounting rules

The financial crisis has brought IFRS and fair value accounting back to the forefront. Prior to 2004, the valuation method for banks' assets was the "historical cost valuation" method. Under this method, the assets retained their original purchase value on the balance sheet, even if their market value had changed in the meantime. In 2004, the so-called Basel II[13] standards were introduced, requiring a change in the method of valuing assets, which will now be the "fair value" method.

The "fair value" or Mark to Market valuation method consists of valuing an asset at its market price. In other words, the reference for the valuation of the assets is the stock market price on the closing date of a company's balance sheet.

This valuation method will be a problem during the crisis: the subprime market collapses and leads to a depreciation of assets in a very short period of time. Banks are obliged to make provisions on these securities and as a result, the balance sheets of financial and banking institutions suffer considerable losses.

To enhance the value of their balance sheets, banks have found a way to divert these new accounting rules. They remove receivables, derivatives containing subprimes, doubtful assets, etc. from their balance sheets. For this purpose, they create SPVs (Special Purpose

---

[13] Basel II standards: see appendix

Vehicles), which are separate legal structures, in which they place these products. When banks were forced to declare these SPVs off-balance sheet and then reintegrate them, this had the effect of revealing huge losses and distorting mutual trust between banks.

4. The role of hedge funds

During this period, hedge funds[14], which engage in short selling, significantly depreciated the shares of financial institutions by massively short selling bank shares, among other things.

SHORT SELLING: the principle is to sell an asset (a stock or an index for example) that you do not yet hold but that you will buy later. The advantage of the operation is to bet (make gains) on the decline in assets. The transaction will be a winner if the investor repurchases the asset at a value lower than the price at which it was sold.

For example, an A share is valued at 10 euros in February. The investor thinks its value will fall, so he will sell it. In March, the buyer's forecast is confirmed, and the action is only worth €7. At this point, the investor buys back the share. The realized capital gain is calculated as follows: 10 - 7 = 3. The gain will therefore be €3 per share.

It should be noted that this type of operation is very risky. Indeed, unlike the traditional purchase, where the loss is limited to the capital invested (if you buy a share €5 and it loses its entire value, you will only lose €5), short selling presents an unlimited risk of loss. Take the previous case: if the value of the A share had risen to €30 in March, the investor would have lost more than his initial capital of €10. Indeed, 10-30= -20, he would not only have lost all his capital (10€), but he would also have had to repay 10€.

Short selling on equities aggravates the financial crisis due to the downward trend in the markets. Indeed, this type of investment makes it possible to achieve positive equity returns in a bear market.

---

[14] Hedge funds: see appendix

As a result, short selling strategies are increasing, causing equity markets to fall more and more and pushing some investors to either sell more to earn more or sell to relieve themselves of the equity risks to which they are exposed.

During the crisis, in an attempt to limit the sharp fall in bank stocks in Europe, short selling was banned.

5. The role of credit rating agencies in the securitization phenomenon

The task of credit rating agencies is to rate bonds in general, and more particularly between 2003 and 2007, bonds issued in exchange for securitized loans (ABS[15] or subprime bonds). These agencies have overrated these bonds, often giving them the highest rating (AAA) to promote their liquidity. Later, when the real estate market started to decline, the agencies did not react quickly enough. Not only did they not lower the ratings of these mortgages when the real estate market turned around to warn of the dangerousness of these products, but they did so in a second phase in a sudden and strong way, which mechanically increased the risk of bondholders and increased distrust towards these products. Some bonds have had their ratings significantly downgraded from AAA to B in a[16] very short period of time. This lack of anticipation had already occurred during the previous crisis, with the bursting of the new technology bubble.

These agencies have played a role in the imbalance in risk distribution among institutions. To maintain low risk, prudential rules require insurers to hold bonds with well-distributed levels of risk in their portfolios. For example, an insurer may have 79% AAA-rated bonds, 10% AA, 10% B, 10% B, and 1% C. Some AAA bonds have been downgraded to BBB, so insurers have been forced to sell them to rebalance the overall risk of the portfolio.

Why didn't the cerdit rating agencies react faster? On the one hand, they did not see the crisis coming, nor did they see its

---

[15] ABS bond: see appendix

[16] See rating system and functioning of credit rating agencies in appendix

magnitude. On the other hand, the rating of these financial products represents a significant part of their turnover, so a deterioration of these products would have negatively impacted their activity.

G7 representatives tried to react to these massive downgrades and subsequently called for more transparency in the work of credit rating agencies.

Here are two concrete examples:

❖ In November 2013, the liquidators of Bear Stearns Bank, which was acquired before Lehman's bankruptcy by JP Morgan, took legal action against the three main credit rating agencies, claiming $1 billion.

❖ In 2012, Australian courts convicted Standard & Poor's of misleading ratings. Indeed, the agency had assigned too high ratings to certain financial assets before the 2008 crisis. The agency then decided to appeal this decision and a new decision was rendered by the Federal Court in June 2014. The court not only dismissed S&P's appeal, but also increased the sentence imposed at first instance.

The facts: in 2006, ABN AMRO bank chose S&P to rate the strength of complex derivatives products called CPDO "Constant Proportion Debt Obligations". S&P rates this product AAA, the highest rating. LGFS, a financial intermediary, then resells this product to municipalities for $16 million. Then, during the financial crisis, S&P downgraded the rating from AAA to BBB, causing the price of this product to collapse. Finally, municipalities were forced to resell these CPDO products with a capital loss of more than 90%.

This conviction by the Australian courts is a world first for a rating agency. Indeed, most lawsuits are filed mainly in the United States. Under normal circumstances, credit rating agencies can hide behind the First Amendment to the US Constitution, which guarantees freedom of expression. However, since freedom of expression is not guaranteed in the same way in the Australian constitution, S&P's defeat was made possible.

27

In 2014, the US Department of Justice is still seeking to recover significant amounts on behalf of investors who have been adversely affected by very generous ratings from S&P before the crisis.

6. Credit enhancers: monoline companies

The monoline is a financial company highly rated by rating agencies (usually AAA) that counter-guarantees an organization or financial asset (often bonds). Through this mechanism, the monoline gives these financial assets the benefit of its excellent financial rating and its advantages in terms of risks and therefore financing.

The monoline Aca Financial has had its rating downgraded from A to CCC (junk bonds) by the rating agency S&P. This reduction resulted in provisions and losses of several billion dollars in the accounts of Crédit Agricole and Merrill Lynch to reflect the deterioration and therefore the unsecured risk of the credit enhancer.

B. The spread of the financial crisis around the world with the crisis of confidence and liquidity

Financial institutions trade billions of dollars every day in financial markets. Similarly, banks lend and sell each other on a daily basis: this is the principle of interbank lending.

The crisis of confidence begins, in part, with the episode of funds called "dynamic money market funds" or "tilted money market funds". These funds are made up of securitized assets, which are highly rated by rating agencies, on the one hand, and traditional monetary assets, on the other. For investors, these assets are therefore considered risk-free. This diversification made it possible to "tilter" performance, i.e. to improve it compared to the performance of a traditional money market fund.

At the beginning of 2007, some of these money products began to react inconsistently by showing significant declines, while money market funds usually do not have volatility[17]. This abnormal

---

[17] Volatility: the magnitude of changes in the price of a financial asset. This makes it possible to assess the risk of a given asset: the larger the variations, the riskier the asset will be.

variation is due to CDO assets[18], which are starting to lose value as a result of massive sales by prudent or informed investors. Due to these strange performances and growing rumors, these money market funds are experiencing very high outflows and are forced to close due to illiquidity of certain assets (these assets no longer find buyers) and to maintain the equality of holders.

After these incidents, banks begin to suspect each other of being contaminated by subprime investments and hesitate to lend to each other as a precautionary measure. Soon, some of them became short of cash and could no longer honor their commitments.

This phenomenon is worsening in parallel with the change in accounting rules: financial institutions are obliged to value their assets at market value (Mark to Market valuation). Faced with this sharp decline in asset valuations, which is increasing as markets decline, mutual trust is disappearing, and the economic losses of financial companies are increasing considerably. The essential ingredient of any market, confidence, is lacking, and the interbank lending market is drying up. Thus, the financial market crisis is rapidly spreading to other sectors and the real economy through the reduction of credit to companies and individuals.

The loss of confidence leads to bank and insurance failures which, forced to declare their off-balance sheet commitments (SPVs, among others), reveal, with Mark to Market valuations, huge losses. Bear Stearns and Lehman are going bankrupt although they are apparently in "good health" and AIG, the largest American insurer, is nationalized in a catastrophe.

In March 2008, the investment bank Bear Stearns was acquired by JP Morgan Chase. On September 15, 2008, investment bank Lehman Brothers, Goldman Sachs' eternal competitor, filed for bankruptcy and filed for protection under Chapter 11 of the US bankruptcy law[19]. On the same date, Bank of America took over

---

[18] CDO: see definition in appendix

[19] "Chapter 11": Chapter 11 of the United States Bankruptcy Act. This chapter provides for a procedure for reorganizing the company in difficulty.

Merrill Lynch, which was about to go bankrupt. These three institutions are victims of the liquidity crisis.

For its part, the American government decided to nationalize the number one insurer in the United States, American International Group, as well as the two main mortgage loan holders Fannie Mae and Freddie Mac. This series of bankruptcies and nationalizations aggravates the situation of confidence and leads to a dramatic fall in financial markets.

The situation continues to worsen until October 2008, mainly due to the crisis of confidence, which leads to the illiquidity of many assets and the need for investors to sell their riskiest assets, whose ratings have deteriorated.

C. The return to growth

To stop the hemorrhaging of financial markets, emerge from the crisis and revive the economy, rescue plans are being launched by governments and central banks on both sides of the Atlantic.

At the same time, most governments around the world are committed to protecting the financial system, stimulating growth and preventing future crises. These guidelines were agreed by the G7 in September 2008 and then by the G20 in the same year.

1. The role of central banks

At the end of 2007, the financial crisis began to gain momentum. Central banks then try to help the various banks by providing them with large amounts of liquidity. Indeed, banks are no longer able to find liquidity on the interbank market due to the crisis of confidence. The Fed and the ECB inject more than 300 billion dollars into the monetary circuit.

How do they do it? Central banks buy back the banks' debts, providing them with currency in exchange. The receivables are then repaid directly to the central banks.

2. Government intervention

In September 2008, in the United States, the Paulson plan or TARP (Trouble Asset Relief Program) was implemented. The purpose of this rescue plan is to create a hive-off vehicle[20] called a "trash bank" or "Bad Bank" and to buy back toxic assets for about $700 billion. The plan also aims to acquire stakes (share purchases) in the major financial companies in Wall Street Square.

Following the launch of this rescue plan, a social protest movement opposing "Main Street" and "Wall Street" emerged. Main Street, a denomination of the American people and more particularly of the taxpayer, demands accounts on the expenses that are made in these companies (about 900 billion dollars) and on the profits that the taxpayer will be able to derive from them. Main Street refuses to pay for the mistakes and abuses of Wall Street "capitalism".

The following month, Europe also carried out a rescue operation. State guarantees are put in place for the refinancing of banks, as well as recapitalization measures. The European Economic Recovery Plan is launched: the European Commission is proposing a package of measures worth €200 billion to support purchasing power and create growth and jobs. Most of these funds (€170 billion) come from national budgets. Across Europe, governments are strengthening the financial soundness of banks by taking stakes, some of which may go as far as nationalization.

In France, in 2008, the State decided to create the Société de Financement de l'Economie Française (SFEF). This company's mission is to finance banks in difficulty by granting them medium and long-term loans. In return, banks are committed to providing more loans to businesses and households in order to boost consumption. Since its creation, SFEF has distributed nearly 80 billion euros on the financial markets and lent about 77 billion euros to banks. Today, in view of the improvement in the banks' situation, SFEF's activity is suspended.

However, by helping banks, governments have considerably increased their public deficits. These negative effects have appeared in several European countries, creating a real contagion phenomenon.

---

[20] Debt relief structure

V. From the subprime crisis to the European debt crisis

A. The structural causes of the European crisis

1. The role of the European Central Bank differs from that of the Fed.

The Fed has three missions: price stability, inflation and unemployment control. Interest rates must help to maintain stable and sustainable economic growth.

In Europe, the ECB has a limited role in defining the monetary policy of the euro area, which is to maintain purchasing power and price stability. This is a rather limited role compared to that of the Federal Reserve. The ECB has also been criticized for not intervening sufficiently in the economy during the financial crises in the euro zone, even if this was not its role. At the time of the crisis, France believed that the ECB should intervene on the markets and buy back government debt. But for Germany, this was not part of its mission. The Lisbon Treaty also proves Germany right: it is prohibited for the ECB to grant credit to a public authority and to directly repurchase debts issued by a country.

2. A lack of a common budgetary, economic or fiscal policy in Europe

There is a fiscal imbalance between euro area countries, with a more advantageous tax rate in some countries: the free movement of capital, products and services is a basic rule of the European market. Companies and individuals can therefore freely choose their location, on which their taxation will depend.

3. A euro too strong in the "southern" countries

The countries of Southern Europe (Greece, Portugal and Spain) suffer from significant external debt due in part to the value of the euro being too high, particularly against the US dollar. In 2010, the euro was overvalued by more than 20% in Greece, Portugal and Spain, but undervalued in Germany and the Netherlands. This euro is "too strong" for the countries of the South, which hinders exports and growth, while growth is stimulated in the countries of the North. This disadvantages exports and favors imports into the South and therefore exports from the North, particularly from Germany. This imbalance contributes to a deterioration in the current account balance and an increase in the debt of the countries of the South, while the opposite phenomenon occurs in the North.

4. A poor appreciation of European interest rates

Northern European countries are more rigorous in their economic policies. Historically, their interest rates have been lower, in line with their financial strength. On the other hand, the countries of the South are less well managed and therefore considered by investors as riskier, their borrowing rates are consequently higher. Thanks to the introduction of the single currency, there has been a convergence of rates, which has enabled the countries of the South to borrow at lower rates. These countries have therefore taken advantage of the situation to borrow more, increasing their debt.

B. The cyclical causes of the crisis

The Euro crisis is, in part, the consequence of the spread of the subprime credit crisis to the global debt market. At that time, American banks, which issue subprime products, sold them worldwide to all financial players, such as banks and insurance companies. The latter are looking for high yields to offset the fall in interest rates, due to the reduction in key rates by the ECB and the Fed[21]. For example, French banks and insurers are adopting these subprime products to improve the performance of euro funds and risk-free products, such as cash and corporate treasury.

The subprime crisis is causing a significant deterioration in public finances in the euro area. States have committed themselves to costly bank bailouts and recovery plans. In 2010, no country in the Eurozone is able to comply with the Stability and Growth Pact[22].

---

[21] See graph on the variation of interest rates

[22] Stability and Growth Pact: see Annex

Between 2007 and 2010, the debt of the euro zone countries increased from 65% to 85% of GDP[23].

The first major event of this period was the Greek and then Irish debt crisis. In the summer of 2011, the various stock market indices fell following the announcement of the size of the Greek debt, which was much higher than expected.

C. The consequences of the crisis

1. Countries in difficulty: PIGS

The crisis particularly affects the countries of the Eurozone, known as "PIGS", which are Portugal, Ireland, Greece and Spain. Italy is sometimes likened to these "PIGS", they are then called "PIIGS". The crisis in the Eurozone really begins with the bankruptcy of Greece.

The most fragile countries in the Eurozone such as Ireland, Spain, Portugal and even Italy are then assimilated to Greece. The approach is not only fundamental but also speculative, since hedge funds[24] take short positions that lower the valuations of these countries' bonds.

Maastricht Treaty: Article 121 of the Treaty establishing the European Community lays down four convergence criteria for the Member States: control of inflation, public debt and public deficit, stability of the unemployment rate and convergence of interest rates.

The thresholds to be respected are as follows:

-The government deficit should not exceed 3% of GDP.

-Public debt must not exceed 60% of GDP.

---

[23] GDP: Gross Domestic Product. According to a definition established by INSEE, it represents the final result of the production activity of the production unit resident in a country.

[24] Hedge funds: see appendix

Difference between public deficit and public debt: the public deficit is the negative annual balance (expenditure being higher than resources) of the general government budget (the State, local authorities, social protection bodies). As for the public debt, it corresponds to the total borrowings contracted by these public administrations.

Euro Zone, 10 Year Treasury Rate Yield

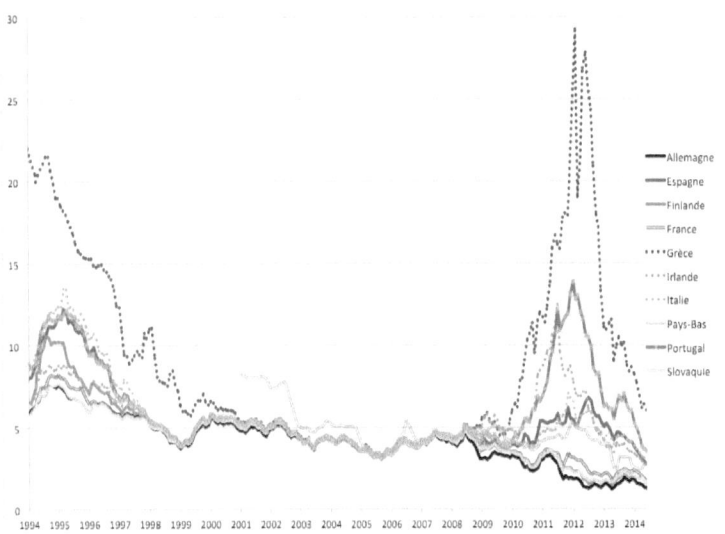

Source : www.ecb.europa.eu

Greece

In November 2009, the new Prime Minister George Papandreou revealed Greece's public deficit: 21.7% of GDP (according to the Maastricht Treaty the deficit must not exceed 3% of GDP), i.e. a deficit 4 times higher than expected by the government. The country then embarked on a period of rigor. The government's statements failed to convince Standard & Poor's, which downgraded the country's rating from A- to BBB+ in December.

In April 2010, after a long period of acute crisis, on the verge of bankruptcy, Greece finally decided to ask for help. Athens obtains a 110-billion-euro loan from the European Union and the IMF in return for a very strict fiscal restraint plan. The Greeks demonstrated, took to the streets, but the government resisted. Anticipating a contagion to other eurozone countries, the zone's leaders are setting up a rescue mechanism of more than 700 billion euros: the European Financial Stability Fund[25] (EFSF). On May 10, the European Central Bank reacted in turn: it repurchased the debt securities of Ireland and Portugal from investors who wanted to get rid of them. The objective is to contain the panic and avoid the contagion of the Greek crisis to the rest of the Eurozone. A temporary calm settles in.

However, on 14 January 2011, the Fitch rating agency in turn placed Greece in the category of issuers in "junk bond" or "rotten debt", further discouraging investors. At the same time, the country, subjected to popular protest, is struggling to implement the rigorous plan promised to the international community. At that time, Greece's public debt reached almost 152% of GDP, whereas the limit set by the Maastricht Treaty is 60%. If Greece had to refinance itself by selling government bonds on the markets, it would have had to pay an interest rate of 12%, four times higher than Germany.

Ireland

The situation in Ireland differs from that in Greece in that the state budget was well controlled until the crisis. For example, in 2007, public debt did not exceed 25% of GDP. It is from 2009 that the country enters into recession: in the first quarter of 2009, the level of GDP was down by 8.5% compared to the first quarter of 2008.

---

[25] EFSF: see paragraph on dealing with the euro area crisis

The Irish debt crisis is initially a private and bank debt crisis... The real estate market, which was in full expansion until 2007, entered a crisis and hit the banking sector hard. When Anglo-Irish Bank came close to bankruptcy, the government decided to nationalize it and provided a guarantee for the entire banking sector. The State thus absorbed the banks' debt and transformed it into public debt. As a result, Ireland's public debt has more than tripled in three years, from 24% of GDP in 2007 to 91% in 2010.

In 2011, the government plans to achieve savings of €15 billion in four years, including €6 billion in the first year. To increase revenues, the government is introducing new taxes and increasing income taxes.

Unemployment reaches a rate of around 14% in 2011, particularly among young people who are increasingly opting for emigration. This weakens domestic demand, but the exporting industry will stimulate economic recovery.

Portugal - Portugal

The eurozone crisis has revealed the weaknesses that Portugal has accumulated over the past ten years. Near-zero growth is characterized by low productivity and derisory wage growth. Investors, frightened by the situation and the risk of bankruptcy in the country, then began to sell their Portuguese debt securities, causing an increase in yield rates.

Why this increase in rates of return? For example, a Greek debt security (bond) is issued at a price of €100, with an interest rate of 5%. This title therefore brings in 5€ per year for the buyer. If debt security holders start selling them, the price will fall, for example to 95€. But the interest rate will remain the same, at 5% of the issue price, so the rate of return for the investor will increase to 5.25%.

Later, these high-risk debt securities will be sought by investors because the European Union, through various mechanisms, will guarantee these securities.

The Fitch rating agency will eventually downgrade Portugal's rating, due to the country's deficit, which is higher than expected and has low growth prospects. In 2009, the country's budget deficit exceeded 9%. Investors no longer see only these defaults, and some are starting to sell their Portuguese debt securities, causing rates to rise. Under these circumstances, the deficit in 2009 is higher than expected and the fragile growth prospects lead the Fitch rating agency to lower the country's rating by one notch to AA.

As a result, austerity measures were adopted by the government: the increase in VAT from 21% to 23%, the increase in income tax, the privatization of certain public companies and the freezing of salaries in the civil service.

At the beginning of May 2011, Portugal is in a bad position and is asking the IMF for help. The socialist government, led by Prime Minister José Socrates, is negotiating an agreement with the delegations of the European Union and the International Monetary Fund. On 4 May, he obtained a loan of €78 billion, including €12 billion to rescue banks in the troubled country.

Spain

Spain joined the European Union in 1986. From that time on, it began a spectacular economic development due in part to the growth of its real estate sector. Compared to other countries in the Eurozone, Spain's public debt is relatively moderate. The main weaknesses of the Spanish economy lie in a high unemployment rate, around 20% (especially among young people) and a sharp fall in house prices, due to the bursting of the housing bubble.

The Spanish economy contracted by 3.7% in 2009 and cannot record positive growth in 2010. In January 2010, Socialist Prime Minister José Luis Zapatero presented a three-year, €50 billion euros plan to reduce Spain's large deficit by 11.1% of GDP. Its objective is to reduce government spending by 4%. The government is trying to raise the retirement age from 65 to 67, triggering mass demonstrations in major cities across the country, but will finally do so in 2011.

The effect of austerity measures disappears due to the lack of growth, the weakening of consumption slows down economic recovery. After five years of crisis, Spain's situation begins to recover in 2014.

Italy

Before the crisis, Italy's public debt was already one of the highest in the entire European Union with more than 100% of its GDP in 2007. This high level of debt is therefore not only due to the crisis in the euro zone but also to an accumulation of previous debts.

Nevertheless, Italy is far from the difficulties affecting the other PIGS countries. The country is coming out of the crisis quite well: even with GDP down by more than 5% in 2009, the real estate market remains stable. One of the reasons for this maintenance is the fact that the majority of the debt is held by Italians and Italian banks.

Regarding the measures to overcome the crisis, in 2011 and 2012 the Italian government drew up a rigorous plan aimed at achieving savings of around €25 billion.

D. Addressing difficulties and emerging from the crisis

The crisis in the euro zone has led to a large number of reforms, which have enabled the most troubled countries to solve some of the older economic problems.

1. Creation of a temporary crisis management mechanism around the European Financial Stability Fund in cooperation with the IMF

On 10 May 2010, the European Union, in cooperation with the IMF, adopted a stabilization fund of over €700 billion. The purpose of this fund is to reassure the financial markets and prevent the Greek crisis from spreading to Spain, Portugal and Italy. Initially endowed with 440 billion euros provided by the States, the fund can be increased to 1,000 billion euros. This amount is borrowed by a

SPV securitization structure[26] and will be used to buy debt from countries in difficulty. The rating agencies give the fund one of the highest ratings. On the same day, the Fed collaborates and opens dollar credit lines to the main central banks of the Western world to prevent them from running out of liquidity. This European Financial Stability Fund will be replaced in 2012 by the Financial Stability Mechanism (FSM).

2. The changing role of the ECB

In May 2010, the ECB authorized central banks to buy back public and private bonds on the secondary markets[27]. In December of the same year, the Governing Council votes on an increase in the ECB's capital.

3. The evolution of the Stability Pact

In March 2011, the finance ministers of the Eurozone countries agreed to reform the Stability Pact in order to strengthen fiscal discipline and avoid excessive debt. Two measures are being taken:

❖   thanks to a set of indicators, the European Commission will be able to alert on imbalances (for example: too high a rise in wages, balance of payments deficit, real estate bubble, etc.),

❖   countries with debt greater than 60% of GDP will have to repay one-twentieth per year of the difference between the total amount of debt and the 60% threshold.

The triggering of sanctions, which was previously the responsibility of local political authorities and subject to the will of States, will be more controlled and automatic in order to increase their credibility.

4. The creation of the pact for the euro

In March 2011, the pact for the Euro was created. This is a coordination between the economic policies of each State. This pact has 4 objectives: to increase economic governance within the

---

[26] Special Purpose Vehicle: see appendix

[27] Secondary markets: see appendix

European Union, to promote competitiveness and convergence within States, to respect the integrity of the single market and to involve the Member States.

These measures are helping the Eurozone to emerge from the crisis. In 2013, even if the various austerity plans remain highly criticized, and growth is low, the overall debt of the euro area is declining for the 2013 budget year (budget implementation year), for the first time since 2007.

Regarding the Greek debt, the government is now showing rather reassuring figures, the country could even post a budget surplus for 2014. But the Greek economy is still stagnating, due to numerous outstanding loans, a recession that has been raging for more than 6 years, and an unemployment rate reaching 28%. On 17 March 2014, Moody's confirmed the AAA rating (maximum rating[28]) of the euro zone and raised the outlook from "negative" to "stable".

Even if the debt crisis seems to have subsided, the Eurozone is not immune to deflation. Fitch points out that "inflation in the euro zone is already the lowest of all the major advanced economies and options for responding to potential deflationary shocks are more limited than elsewhere".

Some economists believe that the Eurozone is moving towards a "Japanicization" of the economy. Indeed, there are signs that the Eurozone could face the same difficulties as Japan in the early 1990s, when the Japanese housing bubble burst[29]. The bursting of this bubble led to a period of economic stagnation and then deflation, with growth stalled for about 20 years. If we analyze the Euro zone at the moment, we can see that it is experiencing some of the same problems as Japan after the housing crash.

---

[28] See the operation of the rating agencies in the appendix

[29] Japanese real estate bubble: see appendix

PART II.

IMPACT OF SIGNIFICANT EVENTS ON FINANCIAL MARKETS

In the first part, the five main trends in financial markets over the past twenty years were presented.

In this second part, the important events of the period will be presented. An analysis of their impact on financial markets will be carried out, whether or not they have contributed to the increase in the level of stress on financial markets and in the media.

❖   Some events had a strong impact on the financial markets:

The bursting of the financial bubble in Thailand, the Asian crisis, the LTCM crisis, on 11 September 2001, the crisis of investor confidence (May to August 2002), the bankruptcy of Lehman Brothers, the announcement of the Paulson plan, the speech by Mario Draghi.

❖   On the contrary, some of them have had little or no influence on the financial markets:

The Fukushima nuclear accident, the declaration of war in Iraq, the devastating hurricane Katrina, the attacks in London, Madrid and Boston.

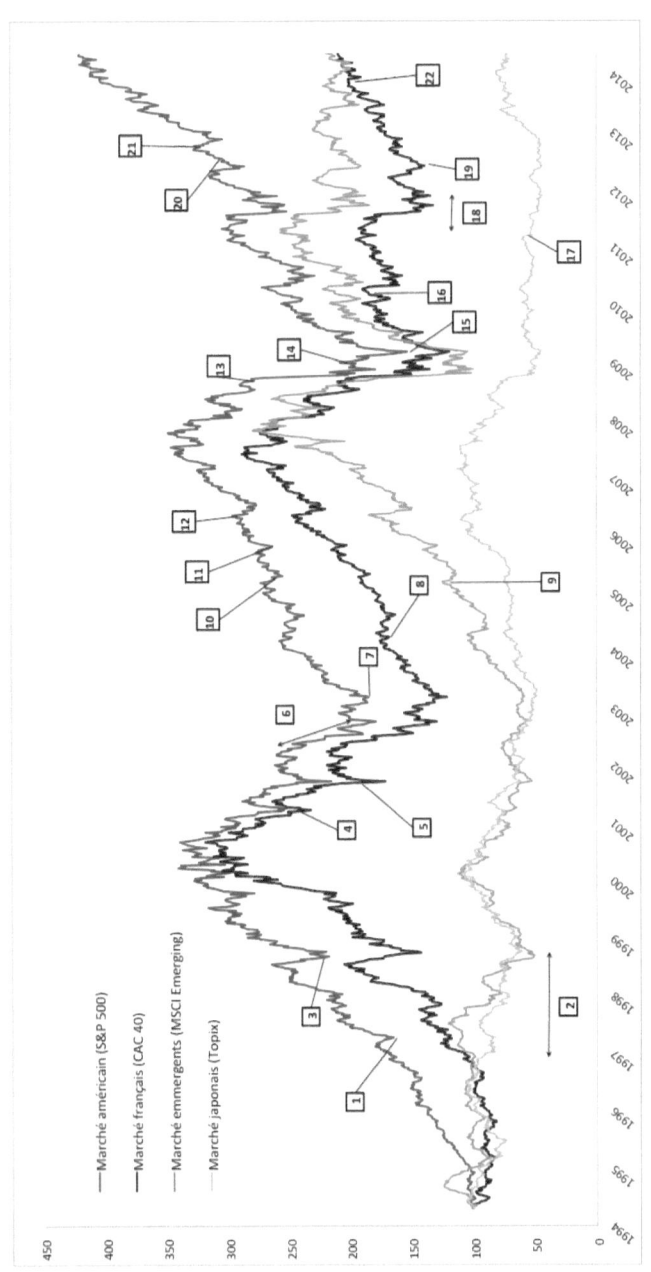

- Marché américain (S&P 500)
- Marché français (CAC 40)
- Marché emmergents (MSCI Emerging)
- Marché japonais (Topix)

Legend

1. Financial bubble burst in Thailand (January 1997)

2. Asian crisis (July 1997 to September 1998)

3. LTCM crisis (23 September 1998)

4. Fall in new technology values (February to March 2001)

5. September 11, 2001

6. Lack of investor confidence (May to August 2002)

7. Declaration of war in Iraq (20 March 2003)

8. Madrid bombings (11 March 2004)

9. Tsunami in South East Asia (26 December 2004)

10. London bombings (July 7, 2005)

11. Hurricane Katrina (late August 2005)

12. Avian influenza (April to July 2006)

13. Bankruptcy of Lehman Brothers (15 September 2008)

14. Paulson Plan Announcement (September 2008)

15. Market Capitulation (March 2009)

16. Degradation of the Greek rating (23 April 2010)

17. Fukushima nuclear accident (11 March 2011)

18. Summer 2011

19. Speech by Mario Draghi (July 26, 2012)

20. Boston Attacks (April 15, 2013)

21. Start of the decrease in Quantitative Easing (QE) in the United States (June 2013)

22. Crimean Crisis (November 2013)

I. Events affecting the financial markets

A. The financial bubble in Thailand

➤ *See point n°1 on the graph*

From the 1960s onwards, Asian countries, particularly Thailand, began to experience strong and sustained economic growth. This growth is driven in particular by the expansion of the production of manufactured products for export.

However, from 1996 onwards, several factors have had an impact on the country's growth development, such as declining exports, currency devaluation, lack of government transparency and poor decisions by financial institutions.

1. The decrease in exports

In 1996, there were first signs of a deterioration in the macroeconomic situation in Thailand. Exports are declining, especially in the textile sector, which will be the most affected. The economic consequences are serious, the authorities and the government refuse to act thinking that this crisis is temporary.

This decline in exports is due to several factors:

❖ Japan, the main importer of Thai products, enters a recession: Japanese demand declines,

❖ Chinese productions are beginning to compete with Thai productions, thanks to cheaper labor.

2. The bursting of the real estate bubble

In 1993, the Thai government established Bangkok International Banking Facilities. It is an offshore financial center that allows[30] foreign investors to invest in Asia through favorable tax rules. Thais are also using it to invest in their own country, fueling a real estate and financial bubble that will burst in the summer of 1997.

---

[30] A legal entity located in a country other than the one in which the activity is carried out, with the aim of optimizing taxation or the financial management of capital.

3. The devaluation of the Baht (Thai currency)

Between 1995 and 1996, the dollar began to rise sharply and appreciated by about 40%. The Thai government is forced to devalue the baht. Thailand's low competitiveness, combined with this depreciation of the baht, leads to a lack of interest from foreign investors who then turn to Laos or Cambodia. On the other hand, investors are discovering that Thailand's short-term debt is higher than its foreign exchange reserves. For fear of the country's bankruptcy, investors are turning to other countries.

4. The government's lack of transparency:

At the same time, political figures showed a lack of transparency regarding the country's economic situation. Indeed, there is a particular economic practice in Thailand: clientelism. This is defined as an unjustified favor granted by politicians to investors in exchange for their votes. This lack of transparency is reinforced by a lack of public communication, official writing and monitoring mechanisms. Under these conditions, it is difficult to regulate the country's economic development.

The Thai government is also responsible for the development of the crisis for another reason: the legislative framework is certainly favorable to economic activities, but the same cannot be said for the parliamentary system. This highly unstable Thai parliamentary system is the source of many coups d'état, reducing investor confidence in the country.

B. The Asian crisis

➢   *See point n°2 on the graph*

The crisis in Thailand, with the bursting of the financial bubble, led to a stock market crisis in early 1997. Investors and financial actors are increasingly suspicious because of the country's excessive short-term debt. Inflation is still high, due to the massive presence of capital that will then flee. This phenomenon of capital flight is compounded by international economic experts, who point out that no international institution wishes to intervene to limit the crisis. For example, the US government refuses to grant Treasury assistance because it considers the difficulties associated with the crisis to be "minor pitfalls". This leads to a general loss of confidence in Asian currencies. Most of these currencies are depreciating, such as the Indonesian rupee and the Philippine peso. The crisis then spread to South Korea, Taiwan, Singapore and Hong Kong in the autumn.

In addition, the situation of local banks and businesses is deteriorating rapidly due to their short-term dollar debt. They then become insolvent. This insolvency, coupled with capital flight, led to a crash in economic activity at the end of 1997. Unfortunately, at that time, countries had great difficulty in exploiting the benefits of the depreciation of their currencies (which were mainly exports at lower cost).

At the end of 1997, 12 emerging countries were affected, including Brazil and Argentina. In October 1997, the Hong Kong monetary authority bought large quantities of shares to support the indices. At the beginning of 1998, the situation improved and deteriorated again because of Indonesia. Indeed, Indonesia is strongly affected by corruption in the banking system, companies and the state. Financial regulation is absent while the country is experiencing a demographic explosion. The crisis leaves a very heavy toll: debt close to 140 billion dollars, inflation of 60%, drop in GDP close to 15%. All this is aggravated by the Suharto plans (President of the Republic of Indonesia from 1967 to 1998), which are incoherent and inadequate: the crisis then becomes political, leading to the resignation of the President.

From spring 1998, the crisis spread to the real economy: the purchasing power of the population declined, and they were no longer able to borrow, due to high interest rates. During the summer, the crisis spread to other emerging countries, such as Russia, causing a crash: the state declared itself in suspension of payment in 1998.

Asian countries, which are suppliers of raw materials and capital goods, are seeing global demand decline: commodity prices are falling, and the crisis then becomes global. But the impact will be short-lived. While Western countries feared a surge in Asian exports to their markets (due to the devaluation of their currencies), the opposite is true, due to low investment and a drying up of available liquidity in these countries. The impact of this crisis therefore remains moderate on a global scale.

C. The LTCM (Long Term Capital Management) crisis

➤ *See point n°3 on the graph*

The LTCM is a hedge fund, created in 1994, whose fall in 1998 affected all international financial markets.

The fund's founder, John Meriwether, gives it a strategy of taking advantage of arbitrage opportunities in interest rate markets with a quantitative approach. The strategy consists in monitoring the differences between actual and estimated theoretical prices and then placing a massive bet on subsequent corrections using leverage[31]. For example, at the end of the century, one of the fund's strategies is based on the convergence of European countries' rates.

Following the Asian crisis, LTCM expects Asian bond rates to return to normal by the end of 1998. But the crisis is spreading to emerging countries, so bond markets are changing in contrast to LTCM's forecasts, which see its capital destroyed in a few days.

On 23 September 1998, as LTCM was about to go bankrupt, a meeting of the presidents of Wall Street investment banks was held with the aim of recapitalizing the fund. Indeed, this fund was then worth nearly 1,200 billion dollars, the equivalent of French GDP. The rumor is worrying and the risks associated with the possible bankruptcy of this fund pose a systemic risk to the global economy.

D. The fall in new technology stocks from February to March 2001

➤ *See point n°4 on the graph*

The simultaneous falls of several large new technology companies caused an exceptional decline in all equity markets from the end of January 2001 to mid-March 2001.

The decline begins with the announcement of poor earnings prospects for some Nasdaq companies, such as Motorola, Sun

---

[31] Leverage effect: see definition in the appendix

Microsystems and Nortel, the telecom equipment giant. Investor sentiment is also affected by the announcement of higher than expected inflation figures in the United States, anticipating an increase in rates often perceived negatively by equity markets.

Monday, March 10, 2003 will be the worst session of the period: the Nasdaq index plunges below the psychological bar of 2000 points (whereas it exceeded 5000 points a year earlier) and loses more than 6%, taking with it the Dow Jones and the Cac 40. This dramatic decline is caused by the latest disappointments in technology stocks, such as Cisco announcing a job cut plan and Ericsson showing poor results.

E. September 11, 2001

➢ *See point n°5 on the graph*

On September 11, four attacks were carried out in the United States a few hours apart and claimed by members of the Islamist terrorist organization al-Qaeda. They target the twin towers of the World Trade Center, the Pentagon, as well as the White House according to the passengers of the fourth plane.

These attacks had a strong but short-lived impact on the various global financial markets. The New York Stock Exchange was closed for four days after the crash of the second plane. Trading in the bond market was also interrupted.

Exchanges only resume the following Monday on Wall Street, September 17. The worst has been avoided: central banks around the world have mobilized and the SEC is exercising its emergency power for the first time to allow companies to buy back their own shares without restriction. The Dow Jones fell by only about 7%, only to return to its pre-attack level just two months later.

F. Lack of investor confidence (May 2002-August 2002)

➢ *See point n°6 on the graph*

From May 2002 onwards, the situation on the financial markets deteriorated. Fears of further attacks, the crisis in the Middle East and the lack of strength of the economic recovery are worrying investors, causing stock market indices to fall. In addition, in June, there was an increase in the number of cases relating to obscure accounting practices and the uncertainties surrounding the debt of major European new technology groups. On June 25, the markets experienced a black day, reaching the stock market levels of September 11, 2001.

In the days that followed, the fall worsened, and the crisis of confidence spread. The irregularities in the accounts of the American company World Com triggered a wave of panic in an economic environment that was already uncertain and weakened a few months earlier by the Enron group case[32].

The crisis continued in July, with the fall of Vivendi Universal and then Alcatel. In mid-July, markets, at their lowest level since 1998, still do not see the end of the tunnel. Each day brings its share of bad news, and discouragement gives way to panic. The crisis will continue until the end of the summer of 2002, when it will ease.

G. Avian influenza (April to July 2006)

➢   *See point n°12 on the graph*

The H5N1 strain of avian influenza virus, which appeared in 2003, killed more than 250 people, mainly in Southeast Asia. In 2006, at the height of the crisis, the International Monetary Fund calculated that an avian influenza pandemic would have a "pronounced but short-lived impact" on the global economy

In 2006, according to WHO (World Health Organization), the development of avian influenza reached the beginning of phase 3, which corresponds to the stage where the influenza virus did not cause human-to-human transmission effective enough to cause a pandemic.

The impacts of avian influenza on the market:

Avian influenza has caused some disorder in the market. Some sectors are affected by the fear of a pandemic, such as airlines, tourism (in a smaller proportion), the agricultural sector (poultry,

---

[32] see paragraph on fraudulent maneuvers in the section on deflating the technology bubble

eggs, livestock, slaughter and processing), as well as activities in close human proximity: leisure, hotels, restaurants, department stores, transport.

Some sectors are taking advantage of this fear, such as the health sector (which will benefit from the expenses generated by the production of treatments to fight the virus) and the communications sector, but a general market decline is nevertheless occurring, especially in emerging countries, which are major poultry consumers.

H. The bankruptcy of the Lehman Brothers bank

➢ *See point n°13 on the graph*

Lehman Brothers was an American bank specializing in investment and corporate banking, headquartered in New York. It went bankrupt on 15 September 2008, during the subprime crisis.

From August 2007, it has been trying to sell its positions in the risky mortgages it held in its portfolio. These subprime positions, which it failed to sell in an environment of mistrust and illiquidity, as well as the freezing of the interbank market, led to its collapse.

In September 2008, the bank asked for government assistance to avoid bankruptcy. At that time of the crisis, the state had already saved several financial institutions such as Fannie Mae and Freddie Mac. Finally, the government refuses to support Lehman Brothers. The bank then declared bankruptcy on 15 September 2008 due to a lack of liquidity and support from the authorities.

The fall of the bank brings with it the American stock exchange and all the world's stock exchanges. The European financial sector is in difficulty, as is AXA, which was Lehman's largest shareholder through its third-party funds.

The collapse of Lehman Brothers was a systemic event for global finance, which has not yet recovered six years later.

I. Paulson Plan Announcement

➢ *See point n°14 on the graph*

The Paulson Plan is a plan put in place by the United States in September 2008 to counter the subprime crisis and the chain failures that threaten the American and global economy. This plan is based on a previously passed law, proposed by Ben Bernanke and Henry Paulson: The Emergency Economic Stabilization Act[33].

Initially, the measures put in place by the plan anticipated that the U.S. Treasury would buy back about $700 billion in "toxic assets" (ABS and CDO bonds[34]). But Henry Paulson reviewed the plan and modified it to directly help companies, so the American treasury took stakes in the capital of some fragile banking groups in order to strengthen their financial strength. However, Congress disagrees on many occasions, due to the prohibitive cost of this plan.

The stock exchanges anticipated the approval of the Paulson plan, adopted on 3 October 2008: there is an increase in the markets, even if the announcement of the plan does not reassure Wall Street, which is waiting to see the effects of the measures on institutions in difficulty. Indeed, after a sharp rise, the market is back on track as of October 6, 2008, due to the succession of defaults announced the previous week. The Paris stock market closed on a fall of more than 9%, its largest daily decline since its creation in 1988. In other European markets, Frankfurt lost 7.07%, London 7.85%. Wall Street opens sharply down, falling below 10,000 points for the Dow Jones.

J. Surrender of markets

➢ *See point n°15 on the graph*

On March 9, 2009, the markets reached their lowest point since 2003 after a spectacular fall. The markets have lost all their bearings and are capitulating. The global crisis is affecting almost all asset classes: equities, corporate bonds, commodities...

On the same day, investors give up and throw in the towel. Why this panic, when governments guarantee deposits and the Paulson plan has been adopted? In this phase of capitulation, a major factor to be taken into account is trust. Banks suspect each other, and

---

[33] Emergency Economic Stabilization Act: see definition in appendix

[34] ABS and CDO bonds: definition in the appendix

savers suspect banks: the money market is frozen. There is panic both for large financial institutions and for small investors, who no longer want to take risks. In England, we saw savers queuing up in front of banks to withdraw their money.

K. Degradation of the Greek note

> ➤ *See point n°16 on the graph*

In spring 2010, European markets are experiencing the first difficulties linked to the European debt crisis. From April 2010, Greece is causing further disruptions in the financial markets, causing the euro to fall below USD 1.33. The Eurozone deficit is rising sharply, and Greece is facing several negative revisions of its deficit, as well as a downgrade in its rating. At the end of April, investors remain nervous due to the failure to repay Greek debt and contamination throughout Europe. In the meantime, Portugal's rating is also downgraded by the S&P agency.

At the end of April 2010, the Paris stock exchange experienced a period of decline, afflicted by investors' fears towards Greece and Portugal. The fall quickly reached Wall Street, after the announcement of another downgrade in the ratings of these two countries. This fear is also aggravated by the uncertainties about the European Union and IMF support plan, linked to Germany's reluctance.

Markets then stagnated and then started to decline again from the end of June 2010. This decline is explained by the fear of economic contagion from the financial sphere. As a result, banks are suffering and Greece is being singled out: the cost of protecting the country against the risk of default is very high, reaching a record high. All this is accentuated by the Fed's negative comments, which herald a difficult economic situation in Europe.

At the end of June 2010, markets are facing an accumulation of bad news, once again undermining investor confidence: Chinese growth, European public debt, bank liquidity. In addition to that, central banks have already done their utmost to try to calm the crisis. Stock markets continue to unscrew, due to worrying economic statistics on growth.

L. Summer 2011

➢ *See point n°18 on the graph*

During the summer of 2011, markets are quite disrupted and are dropping dramatically. Fear of a global recession is the catalyst.

Summer 2011 is a time of concern: growth has remained very modest since 2009 in the United States, where GDP has fallen by almost two and a half percentage points. Concerning Europe, Spain is suffering from the deflation of its real estate bubble, and Greece is still in great difficulty: in general, growth is very weak in Europe.

As for the financial context, it is favorable to a downward trend. Banks have faced huge losses due to the subprime crisis, and their already fragile situation is aggravated by the fall in the value of Greek bonds. In addition to all this, there is one last important factor: major financial institutions are the subject of rumors about their financial health, particularly in France.

A sharp decline begins at the end of July 2011, based on the following factors:

❖ the vote on the Europe Agreement on aid to Greece on 20 July: eurozone leaders vote on an aid plan for Greece, providing €158 billion in aid. Oppositions to this plan have taken place between France and Germany. At the same time, Moody's, in doubt, places Spain under surveillance because of its large budget deficit and almost zero growth in 2010,

❖ Spanish debt under surveillance: Moody's, which had already downgraded Spain's rating from Aa1 to Aa2 in March, plans to renew the operation on 29 July 2011. It justifies its decision by noting that Spain has difficulties in enforcing budgetary discipline and that the economic context created by the announcement of Greece's rescue plan increases the risk for investors holding public bonds,

❖ Credit credit rating agency are reacting to the increase in the US debt ceiling by Congress: this increase is essential to pay officials in July. Investors doubt that this measure will produce a real and significant reduction in the deficit. Finally, the rating agency S&P

downgrades the rating of the United States, which is losing its AAA rating - still unthinkable a few years ago - and which is the real detonator of this crisis,

❖   Rumors about banks: in mid-August, a large number of French banks were the subject of erroneous statements. The most alarmist concerns Société Générale, through the publication of an article in a London tabloid stating that the bank is on the verge of disaster, after huge losses. Despite the newspaper's denial of this information, other rumors are spreading, investors fear that France will lose its AAA,

❖   a confirmed economic slowdown: the publication of the figures for the various European GDPs, starting in mid-August, shows a sharp economic slowdown. These figures also reflect the spread of gloom, particularly in the service sector. Morgan Stanley Bank forecasts economic growth of less than 0.5% in the euro zone in 2012, compared to its initial forecast of +1.2%.

M. Speech by Mario Draghi President of the European Central Bank (ECB)

➢   *See point n°19 on the graph*

In a context of crisis and heightened doubt, the new President of the ECB, Mario Draghi, speaks out on the rescue of the euro by the ECB in a speech on 26 July 2012.

All markets were waiting for it: "*The ECB (...) is ready to do whatever it takes to preserve the Euro. And believe me, it will be enough*". With these few words, Mario Draghi implies that the ECB will be able to buy back the government bonds on the secondary market that had dried up since February.

The impact of this speech was to reassure all stock markets, which have been in a gloomy state for more than a year. The CAC 40 gained more than 4% in one day and Spain's 10-year borrowing rate fell considerably: it fell below 7%, whereas it was close to 8% a few days earlier. After the ECB announced the rescue of the euro, the market is back on the rise once and for all.

N. Reduction of Quantitative Easing - QE

> ➤ *See point n°21 on the graph*

Quantitative Easing is a "non-conventional" monetary policy conducted by the US central bank since the end of 2010. The EQ mechanism can be described as follows: after approval by the Treasury, the Central Bank creates money. But this currency is not physically created by the central bank, it is only a line of credit on its account. In order to inject the newly created money into the economy, the central bank then buys sovereign bonds (government bonds) from banks and insurance companies. These institutions therefore have new liquidity, which they will be able to lend to households and businesses, which will promote consumption and boost growth. Once the growth target is reached, the central bank must (in theory) sell its good sovereigns and then destroy the currency it has created, thus avoiding inflation.

Quantitative Easing is essential to boost growth following a crisis. But central banks cannot continue to provide liquidity forever, they must reduce the amount of liquidity injected over time. On 19 June 2013, Ben Bernanke, Chairman of the Fed[35], announced that the Fed's liquidity injections could slow down from the end of 2013, to stop completely in 2014.

Investors reacted quickly: this announcement, combined with the publication of bad PMI[36] in China, led to a sharp drop in markets.

---

[35] Fed: Federal Reserve System, U.S. central bank, definition in appendix

[36] The PMI, "Purchasing Managers Index", is the indicator of activity in the manufacturing sector. It is calculated after a monthly survey of purchasing managers in the industry and gives an immediate picture of the health of manufacturing activity.

II. Significant events that did not impact the financial markets

Some major events, such as natural disasters or major political events, have had little or no impact on financial markets.

A. The declaration of war in Iraq

➢ *See point n°7 on the graph*

On March 20, 2003, the United States declared war on Iraq. If financial markets were initially tense, due to the uncertainties surrounding this conflict, it took a few weeks for the situation to calm down.

There was a slight drop in the market, particularly on 25 March 2003: the Dow Jones index fell by 3.61%, due to Iraq's resistance and George Bush's request for a budget extension to finance the war.

But due to the positive turn of events in the conflict, investors will regain confidence and the market will quickly recover. Finally, further deterioration of the situation in Iraq will not be a concern for investors. "The market, very optimistic, now prefers to listen to the good economic news rather than worry about the slow escalation of international tensions," says Jean-Pierre Petit, Exane's Chief Economist. For him to come back to the Iraqi issue, this economic optimism would have to suffer from some disappointments. »

B. The attacks in Madrid, London and Boston

➢ *See points 8, 10 and 20 on the graph*

❖ The Madrid bombings

The Madrid attacks, claimed by Islamist extremists on 11 March 2004, killed nearly 1,600 people. These bomb attacks, condemned by the international community as an act of terrorism, are the most significant in Europe since 1988.

European stock markets fell as the news broke. In Paris, the same day, the CAC 40 index fell by nearly 3%, fearing that al-Qaeda would be the instigator of these attacks. The transport and tourism sectors are severely affected. But a few days later, the French, German and English markets recovered, and then Spain quickly followed. The few fears of investors still present will finally dissipate a week later after the Fed announced that its rates would remain at 1%.

❖   The London bombings

The London bombings were committed by four British Islamist terrorists on 7 July 2005 on London public transport, killing 56 people and injuring 700.

In a climate of fear, the CAC 40 fell by nearly 2.5% on the day of the attacks, while the Footsie lost nearly 3.5%. But losses remain very limited and the London Stock Exchange will recover after only one day. The effect of the London attacks on markets is much less than the attacks of 11 September or Madrid the previous year. It can be seen that market resistance to terrorist acts has increased since 11 September.

❖   The Boston bombings

On April 15, 2013, during the Boston Marathon, two bombs exploded near the finish line, killing 3 people and injuring more than 260 others.

On the day of the attack, the New York Stock Exchange fell, followed by the Asian stock exchanges. In addition, these attacks come at a time of decisive discussions on the US budget, aggravating the decline. However, markets regained stability soon after the attack.

C. Tsunami in Southeast Asia

➢   *See point n°9 on the graph*

It is one of the worst natural and humanitarian disasters in a century. On 26 December 2004, the tsunami struck Malaysia, Thailand, Sri Lanka and India. The death toll is very high: about 220,000 deaths according to the UN.

However, there was no change in the financial markets: the MSCI Emerging markets stock market index did not fall. The explanation for this lack of variation is based on the limited economic importance of this area. The areas affected are mainly rural areas and beaches, without companies and large cities.

D. Hurricane Katrina

➢   *See point n°11 on the graph*

At the end of August 2005, Hurricane Katrina, one of the most powerful hurricanes in US history, struck almost the entire Gulf of Mexico and several American states were affected: Louisiana, Mississippi and Alabama. Some cities are suffering enormous damage, such as New Orleans, where more than 200,000 houses have been destroyed. The hurricane would go so far as to cause significant damage in Quebec, on the east coast of Canada.

This disaster, which was a shock for the United States, had no impact on the financial markets. The New York Stock Exchange is holding up very well, with a slight increase. Why? The affected areas represent only 3% of the United States' GDP. Although US growth will decline slightly, once the recessionary shock is over, growth will resume thanks to the country's planned reconstruction efforts.

Source : National hurricane center

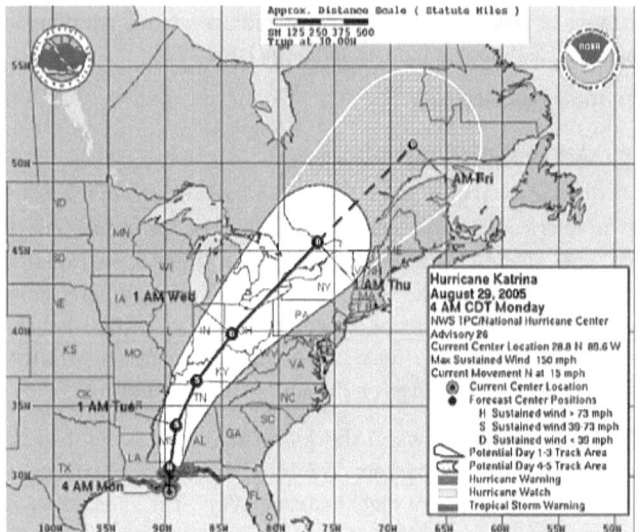

Source : National hurricane center

E. The Fukushima nuclear accident

➤ *See point n°17 on the graph*

The Fukushima nuclear accident occurred on March 11, 2011 in Japan. It is a major nuclear accident classified at level 7, the highest on the International Nuclear Events Scale. In comparison, the Chernobyl accident in 1986 was also classified as a level 7 accident.

This accident had only a limited influence on the Japanese market and its influence is almost non-existent in other world markets. Why? Japan accounts for only 0.1% of world growth. The reconstruction of the area after the accident even had a positive impact on the country's growth, which represents only 3% of Japanese GDP.

As with the two previous events (Tsunami of 2004 and Hurricane Katrina), the affected area is not a major economic area, so the financial impact is low.

F. Crimean annexation

> ➢ *See point n°22 on the graph*

In November 2013, Ukraine refused to ratify the association treaty with the European Union in order to relaunch its economic relations with Russia. The Treaty provided for a political and economic association between Ukraine and Europe through common economic legislation and rules. Following this refusal, many demonstrations took place in the country, particularly in Kiev, with the occupation of the central square: "Maïdan Nézalejnosti" (Independence Square). The main demand is the resignation of President Viktor Yanukovych. Subsequently, other large-scale armed events and demonstrations will take place to lead to the annexation of Crimea by Russia.

The impact of this conflict on financial markets remains limited. Indeed, even if this country of 45 million inhabitants is as vast as France, its GDP is 20 times smaller.

ANNEX

ABS: Asset Backed Securities. This is the basic principle of transforming an asset, often tangible, into a negotiable security. We can securitize real property such as an aircraft or the copyrights of a book, for example.

Credit rating agencies: A rating agency is a company or institution responsible for the financial rating of public authorities, governments or private companies.

The main credit rating agencies:

❖ *Standard & Poor's (USA Nationality), a* member of the McGraw-Hill Group, also known in the US market for its stock market indices such as the S&P 500, which represents the entire US economy.

❖ *Moody's (Nationality USA) is a* publicly traded company specializing in the provision of integrated risk management, financial analysis and rating solutions.

❖ *Fitch Ratings (French nationality)*, 60% owned by Fimalac Financial Holding.

❖ *Dagong (*Chinese nationality) is a recent agency in the economic landscape. Its ratings have less impact on the markets than the three previous agencies.

The agencies rate companies for a fee, their clients are private companies but also public authorities. Their independence has been increasingly discussed since the accounting manipulation case and the financial crisis from 2007 to 2011. Indeed, many investors complain about the lack of transparency, responsiveness, rating methods and potential conflicts of interest that exist.

<u>Examples of the limits of the agency and rating system</u>:

❖ during the subprime crisis, major credit rating agencies often give CDO-type investments the highest rating, which implies that their risk is extremely low in the medium and long term. The fall in real estate and the failure to repay loans quickly swings the risk, forcing credit rating agencies to downgrade the ratings of these financial products, resulting in losses for investors,

❖ before the financial crisis, a significant proportion of the credit rating agencies' income comes from the rating of securitized products, creating doubts about a possible conflict of interest. The sovereignty of rating agencies is being questioned, and some companies are even refusing to be rated so that they do not have to report to the agencies,

❖ On the eve of its bankruptcy, Lehman Brothers is rated in Investment Grade (high rating), i.e. with very low risk,

❖ on November 10, 2011, in the midst of the eurozone debt crisis, an email was sent by mistake by the S&P agency announcing the downgrade of France's rating. Two hours later a patch cancels this announcement. On June 3, 2014, ESMA (the European Securities and Markets Authority) blamed S&P for this error. It considers that this erroneous announcement is the result of breaches in compliance with the control procedures that the rating agency has put in place.

Meaning of the note		Moody's		Standard & Poor's		Fitch Ratings		Dagong	
		Long term	Short-term	LT	TC	LT	TC	LT	TC
INVESTMENT CATEGORY	First one quality	Aaaa	P-1	AAA	A-1+	AAA	F1+	AAA	A-1
	High quality	Aa1		AA+		AA+		AA+	
		Aa2		AA		AA		AA	
		Aa3		AA-		AA-		AA-	
	Higher average quality	A1		A+	A-1	A+	F1	A+	
		A2		A		A		A	
		A3	P-2	A-	A-2	A-	F2	A-	A-2
	Lower average quality	Baa1		BBB+		BBB+		BB+	
		Baa2	P-3	BBB	A-3	BBB	F3	BBB	A-3
		Baa3		BBB-		BBB-		BBB-	
SPECULATIVE CATEGORY	Speculative	Ba1		BB+	B	BB+	B	BB+	B
		Ba2		BB		BB		BB	
		Ba3		BB-		BB-		BB-	
	Very speculative	B1		B+		B+		B+	
		B2		B		B		B	
		B3		B-		B-		B-	
	High risk	Caa1	Not bonus	CCC+	C		C		C
	Ultra speculative	Caa2		CCC		CCC		CCC	
	In default, with some hope of recovery	Caa3		CCC-					
		This		CC		CC		CC	
				C		C		C	
	In selective default	C		SD	D	D	D	D	D
	In default			D					

Japanese Real Estate Bubble: The Japanese Real Estate Bubble is an economic and financial bubble that formed in Japan from 1986 to 1990. Since 1986, Japanese real estate prices have been rising, especially in the commercial sector. This price increase is much higher than inflation, and mainly affects the six main cities.

In 1990, prices began their downward phase, the bubble deflated. This deflation, initially modest, will accelerate during 1992 and will only stop after 15 years of consecutive declines in 2005. The bursting of this bubble is accompanied by the fall of Japanese stock market indices, with a low in 2003 and a long period of deflation.

ECB: it is the Central Bank of the European Union, based in Frankfurt. It was created on the 1st of June 1981 and its mission is to define the monetary policy of the Euro zone, to maintain purchasing power and price stability.

CDO: Collateralized Debt Obligation. These are asset-backed bonds: a category of ABS made up of bank and corporate debt. There are different levels of risk on these assets, depending on the issuer of the debt.

Leverage effect: Leverage effect is a mechanism that multiplies exposure to a financial asset, and therefore performance in the same proportion, whether negative or positive.

Emergency Economic Stabilization Act: commonly referred to as the U.S. financial system rescue plan, it is a law passed in response to the subprime crisis, authorizing the U.S. Treasury Secretary to spend up to $700 billion to buy questionable assets, particularly mortgage-backed securities, directly from banks.

Fannie Mae: abbreviation of the Federal National Mortgage Association. A company created by the United States federal government to make the mortgage market liquid. In practice, it is authorized to lend and guarantee loans to other financial institutions, such as banks.

Freddy Mac: abbreviation for Federal Home Loan Mortgage Corporation (FHLMC). Company created under the same conditions and for the same purpose as Fannie Mae. Freddy Mac buys mortgages, assembles them and sells them to investors in the global market.

In 2008, Fannie Mae and Freddy Mac guaranteed or owned more than $5 trillion in mortgages, or about 40% of all loans granted in the United States. They will be hit very hard by the subprime crisis.

Fed "Federal Reserve System": is the central bank of the United States. It was founded by Congress in 1913 to create a flexible and stable monetary and financial system. The Fed's objective is to define the United States' monetary policy by controlling interest rates, unemployment and price stability. It also regulates the financial system to protect consumer rights and ensure banking security. Finally, its role is also to maintain the stability of the financing system and to contain systemic risks that could arise in financial markets.

Hedge funds: These funds use management strategies that must produce a performance that is often absolute and uncorrelated to the financial markets. Strategies (long short equity, global macro, etc...) have a low to very high-risk level. The limit is the transparency of management. For example, the Madoff fund was a hedge fund whose scam was highlighted during the 2008-2009 financial crisis. It's very efficient and constant management was a fraudulent financial arrangement based on the Ponzi scheme.

Secondary market: The primary market is distinguished from the secondary market. The latter connects buyers and sellers of securities already issued. Once a company has issued shares or debt on the primary market, these securities can then be traded freely on the secondary market between investors.

NASDAQ: NASDAQ is the abbreviation for "National Association of Securities Dealers Automated Quotations". It is the second largest equity market in the United States, after the NYSE (New York Stock Exchange), in terms of volume traded. He is specialized in the technology stocks sector.

Basel II and Basel III standards: These standards form prudential mechanisms designed to anticipate banking risks and more particularly credit risk. They provide a minimum level of equity capital to ensure financial security. Basel standards are guidelines created since 1988 by the Basel Committee.

Stability and Growth Pact: The Stability and Growth Pact (SGP) was concluded between the countries of the euro zone in order to coordinate their fiscal policies. The PSC requires the countries of the zone to eventually have surplus budgets, or if not close to balance. The SGP was adopted at the Amsterdam European Council in 1997 and includes two types of measures:

❖ Multilateral surveillance, a preventive measure: it is an alert system that allows the Ecofin Council (comprising the EU's Ministers of Economy and Finance) to make a recommendation to a country that is not respecting its obligations,

❖ the excessive deficit procedure, a deterrent measure: if a country has a public deficit that is too high and exceeds the 3% of GDP criterion, the ECOFIN Council makes a recommendation to the country. If the State does not react, the Council may impose sanctions: a fine may be imposed on the State, which must pay the ECB an amount ranging from 0.2 to 0.3% of its GDP.

SPV "Special Vehicle Funds": It is a securitization vehicle, bringing together illiquid bank loans in order to issue shares or bonds that can be resold more easily on the market.

Stock options: A stock option is a call option issued by a company whose underlying asset is its share. Holders of stock options can then purchase shares of the company on a date and at a price fixed in advance. This system allows buyers to benefit from a lower price than the market, and to realize a significant capital gain on resale.

Securitization: banks, which issue loans, create intermediary companies in which these loans constitute assets. In return for these assets, the bank issues bonds, which constitute the liabilities of these intermediary companies. The interest and loan repayments are then used to pay interest on the bonds issued and to repay them. The main interest of securitization is to monetize (make liquid and exchangeable) initially illiquid private and commercial movable assets.

TABLE OF CONTENTS

PART I. INFLUENCE OF MAJOR ECONOMIC TRENDS ON FINANCIAL MARKETS   7

I. OF THE NEW ECONOMY TO   7
THE CREATION OF THE INTERNET BUBBLE   7
A. THE BEGINNINGS OF THE DEVELOPMENT OF THE INTERNET BUBBLE   8
B. FACTORS DRIVING THE DEVELOPMENT OF THE INTERNET BUBBLE   9
II. THE DEFLATION OF THE TECHNOLOGY BUBBLE   11
A. COURSE OF EVENTS   11
1. The runaway phase (fall 1999 - spring 2000)   11
2. The doubt phase (spring to autumn 2000)   11
3. The stagnation phase (November 2000 - November 2001)   12
4. The panic phase (from December 2001 to February 2003)   13
B. FACTORS AGGRAVATING THE CRISIS   14
1. Major fraud schemes   14
2. The crash of financial analysts   15
III. CREATION OF THE FINANCIAL BUBBLE   18
A. THE RETURN TO GROWTH OF FINANCIAL MARKETS   18
B. THE CREATION OF THE REAL ESTATE BUBBLE IN THE UNITED STATES   19
IV. THE SUBPRIME CRISIS AND THE DEFLATION OF THE BUBBLE   22
A. THE CAUSES OF THE SUBPRIME CRISIS   22
1. The rise in interest rates initiated by the Fed   22
2. Securitization of receivables   23
3. The change in accounting rules   24
4. The role of hedge funds   25
5. The role of credit rating agencies in the securitization
phenomenon   26
6. Credit enhancers: monoline companies   28
B. THE SPREAD OF THE FINANCIAL CRISIS AROUND THE WORLD WITH THE CRISIS
OF CONFIDENCE AND LIQUIDITY   28
C. THE RETURN TO GROWTH   30
1. The role of central banks   30
2. Government intervention   30
V. FROM THE SUBPRIME CRISIS TO THE EUROPEAN DEBT CRISIS   32
A. THE STRUCTURAL CAUSES OF THE EUROPEAN CRISIS   32
1. The role of the ECB differs from that of the Fed.   32
2. A lack of a common budgetary, economic or fiscal policy in
Europe   32

3. A euro too strong in the "southern" countries   32
4. A poor appreciation of European interest rates   33
B. THE CYCLICAL CAUSES OF THE CRISIS   33
C. THE CONSEQUENCES OF THE CRISIS   34
1. Countries in difficulty: PIGS   34
D. ADDRESSING DIFFICULTIES AND EMERGING FROM THE CRISIS   39
1. Creation of the European Financial Stability Fund   39
2. The changing role of the ECB   40
3. The evolution of the Stability Pact   40
4. The creation of the pact for the euro   40

**PART II. IMPACT OF SIGNIFICANT EVENTS ON FINANCIAL
MARKETS**   **42**

I. EVENTS AFFECTING THE FINANCIAL MARKETS   **45**
A. THE FINANCIAL BUBBLE IN THAILAND   45
1. The decrease in exports   45
2. The bursting of the real estate bubble   45
3. The devaluation of the Baht (Thai currency)   46
4. The government's lack of transparency: 46
B. THE ASIAN CRISIS   46
C. THE LTCM (LONG TERM CAPITAL MANAGEMENT) CRISIS   48
D. THE FALL IN NEW TECHNOLOGY STOCKS FROM FEBRUARY TO MARCH 2001   48
E. SEPTEMBER 11, 2001   49
F. LACK OF INVESTOR CONFIDENCE (MAY 2002-AUGUST 2002)   49
G. AVIAN INFLUENZA (APRIL TO JULY 2006)   50
H. THE BANKRUPTCY OF THE LEHMAN BROTHERS BANK   51
I. PAULSON PLAN ANNOUNCEMENT   51
J. SURRENDER OF MARKETS   52
K. DEGRADATION OF THE GREEK NOTE   53
L. SUMMER 2011   54
M. SPEECH BY MARIO DRAGHI PRESIDENT OF THE EUROPEAN CENTRAL BANK   55
N. REDUCTION OF QUANTITATIVE EASING - QE   56
II. SIGNIFICANT EVENTS THAT DID NOT IMPACT THE FINANCIAL MARKETS   **57**
A. THE DECLARATION OF WAR IN IRAQ   57
B. THE ATTACKS IN MADRID, LONDON AND BOSTON   57
C. TSUNAMI IN SOUTHEAST ASIA   58
D. HURRICANE KATRINA   59
E. THE FUKUSHIMA NUCLEAR ACCIDENT   60
F. CRIMEAN ANNEXATION   61

ANNEX   **62**

www.ingramcontent.com/pod-product-compliance
Lightning Source LLC
Chambersburg PA
CBHW020707180526
45163CB00008B/2975